P.E.N. BOOKS

THOMAS HARDY

P.E.N. BOOKS

P.E.N. BOOKS

General Editor: Hermon Ould

THOMAS HARDY

by

Henry W. Nevinson

London

George Allen & Unwin Ltd

FIRST PUBLISHED IN 1941
SECOND IMPRESSION IN 1943

PRINTED IN GREAT BRITAIN
in 11-Point Perpetua Type
BY UNWIN BROTHERS LIMITED
WOKING

CONTENTS

WHEN the Executive of the London P.E.N. Club in 1940 were planning a series of short volumes to be written by members of the Club, the Editor suggested that I should do one on Thomas Hardy. His reason was that I had known him personally, and for a few years had even been honoured by his friendship. I knew that it would be impossible to say half that I should wish to say about a great and famous writer, so imaginative and fertile, and it has been impossible. I have been obliged to follow the main subjects only, and, under that strict limitation, I have divided the given length into the four chapters—personal memories, the stories (for his own works he objected to the word "novels"), his poems, and "The Dynasts." Even among his stories I have limited myself to the four that seem to me the chief, while I have omitted the shorter scenes and sketches, admirable as some of them are for their humour and irony.

I have throughout followed the guidance of my own opinion or appreciation, avoiding the natural enthusiasm that may misguide, and even more the supercilious contempt which has of recent years been exuding its slime over Hardy as over so many of the great characters and writers of the last century.

I gratefully acknowledge three debts. One night, early in this century, when I was leader-writing, or editing the literary page of the old *Daily Chronicle* in Whitefriars Street, a messenger-boy came hurriedly into my room, saying that the police had found an unknown man lying badly hurt on the pavement outside, and the only document discovered on him was a letter addressed to me. At the top of the street, near the entrance from Fleet Street, I saw a man lying with blood pouring from his head, and the usual crowd looking on. He was Lionel Johnson, true poet, and the very best of the distinguished critics whom I had collected to write for my "Page". In his pocket was a review he was bringing to me when he must have slipped or been pushed so that he struck his head violently on the stones. We conveyed him to "Bart's" and they laid him on a bed where he remained breathing with a snoring sound, as patients with broken skulls do. The doctor told me the skull was unusually thin and breakable. Johnson died that night, and we buried him in Kensal Green Cemetery —a man of perhaps over-sensitive nature, imaginative, a master of English, a faultless critic, writing a beautiful hand with hardly ever a correction, one of the very few among my reviewers whose "copy" I could send up without reading it, for it was sure to be right.

In 1894 he published "The Art of Thomas Hardy" (Elkin Mathews and John Lane). It is a model of appreciative criticism, full of thought and unusual knowledge, especially of Greek, Roman, and Italian literature. It was published in the same year as "Life's Little Ironies" and six years before the complete edition of "The Dynasts" (1910).

Last year (1940) Mr. G. M. Young published "Selected Poems of Thomas Hardy" (Macmillan). No anthology will ever please everyone, least of all those who have some acquaintance with the main body from which the selection is made. But in this selection I have noticed the absence of only one poem which I should have included. I am also grateful for the author's Introduction, in which he writes much that is valuable upon poetry in general, the influence of place upon Hardy, and the whole tendency of the poet's mind. But he is not too lost in admiration to admit that sometimes in Hardy's poems "All the Muses hold their ears in pain".

In the third place I should notice "An Anthology of Modern Verse" (Methuen's English Classics), chosen by A. Methuen, and containing a very remarkable Introduction on Poetry by Robert Lynd. The book is dedicated to "Thomas Hardy, O.M. Greatest of the Moderns", and includes a brief but excellent selection of his poems.

H. W. N.

IN EXILE AT CAMPDEN, GLOS.

January 1941

CHAPTER I

Thomas Hardy (1840–1928)

AS I KNEW HIM

WHEN first I met Thomas Hardy he was already sixty-three, and the great series of his prose works was completed. From what I had read of his passionate love for the Wessex country and the country people, I had expected to find a bronzed and stalwart countryman, vigorous, and redolent of country life. Very different was my first impression. I had been invited to stay for a few days at Aldeburgh on the Suffolk coast with that fearless and sceptical thinker, Edward Clodd, a distinguished banker, better known among scientific people as a student of Folklore, and to myself as "the friend of genius and the genius of friendship", to use my own description of him. For Clodd had a lovable way of gathering his friends around him for his brief holidays in a rambling, shiplike house overlooking the brown North Sea. George Meredith was often there, and Professor Haddon the anthropologist, and Sir James Frazer of the "Golden Bough", and Flinders Petrie, the explorer of ancient Egypt, and Hugh Clifford of the Malay Peninsula, and James Cotton with his knowledge of India, and Sir Louis Dane of Cabul, and General John Seely (Lord Mottistone): but the full list would be too long. To myself Thomas Hardy on our first meeting was by far the most attractive and interesting figure.

Also the most unexpected in appearance. He was not large

or countrified or robust. He was spare and straight in figure, hands white and soft and loose-skinned, face grey-white like delicate wax, lined with thin wrinkles, thoughtful and pathetic and profoundly sad, showing little of power or rage or physical courage; eyes bluish-grey, already whitening, head rather bald, but fringed with soft light hair, the eyebrows and moustache of the same colour and thin texture. He sat quite silent at first, and took little notice of the conversation. Then he began to talk, always with simple and quite unconscious modesty, attempting no phrase or eloquence such as Meredith delighted in, but just stating his opinion or telling some reminiscence or story—always a little shyly like a country cousin among quick-witted Londoners. Indeed, at a later meeting he told me that when among Londoners he at first felt overcome by their wit and knowledge, but afterwards he perceived that they usually had only three ideas which they repeated.

He spoke of his early days in Dorset when life was so much fuller and more various than now, chiefly owing to the system of holding cottages on three lives—"liviers" the tenants were called—which gave them a permanency and personal interest in the place. Now, the Cockney's idea that all country people are agricultural labourers is almost true. He himself was born only just in time to catch the relics of the older days.

As I expected, he spoke much about hangmen; also about the horrible scenes at public floggings on a waggon in the market-place, and how cruel hangman would wait between each lash to let the flesh recover its feeling, while he squeezed the blood off the thongs, and how some soldiers once noticed this and forced the man to go quicker; and how, before his time, children used to be flogged through the streets behind a cart for stealing a penny book or toy. He had stories of magic as well; of the woman who dreamt another woman sat on her chest and clawed her arm, and that other woman came next day to be healed of a terrible red mark on her arm of which she ultimately died. He said he had written a story on it for Leslie Stephen, who, however, insisted upon having a material explanation. He told also of the custom still surviving that the man who kills a pig cuts out a little piece and eats it raw. With a naïve gesture he imitated the action of the man eating it. This of course, roused the others to scientific discussion on the rites of propitiation; for Haddon was there, bubbling over with Primitive Culture.

I met Hardy again at Clodd's in 1905 when a few of us were gathered in Aldeburgh to celebrate the hundred-and-fiftieth year after the poet George Crabbe's birth in the old town. Hardy, who had studied Architecture early for his profession, as is evident in so many of his works, and was always deeply interested in the buildings of the English Church, went to the commemoration services in the ancient church, because, as he told me, he honoured in Crabbe the first of the Realists, and that stern poet had held his first curacy there. Early in the next year, as I was sitting in the pit at Terry's Theatre in the Strand to see Maxim Gorky's satiric play, "The Bezsemenoffs", Hardy came creeping in and sat beside me. He was in his usual mood, gentle, sensible, unpretentious. He thought some guide-books then appearing on Wessex might advertise his own works a little! He talked of "The Dynasts", and mentioned the futility of American criticism, which always waits to see what English critics say before it dares express an opinion. He said that "Tess" had sold best of his works, and "Far from the Madding Crowd", next best. He enjoyed concerts better than theatres, and thought Tchaykovsky's music exactly expressed the modern tone of unrest. Best of all he liked to go to St. Paul's to hear the chanting, always choosing out his favourite chants according to the day's programme. After the theatre we went to a Lyons' tea-shop at which he was a little alarmed, being used only to an A.B.C., and unfortunately, as we came out, he caught sight of a broadsheet, announcing "Family murdered with a Penknife!" He could not get over that penknife, and kept on repeating the word. So we parted amiably in the Strand, the passers-by remaining quite unconscious how great a man moved among them.

But my own most intimate acquaintance with that sensitive and deeply poetic spirit came in 1906 when he invited me to visit him in his home at Dorchester. The pleasant house of Max Gate stood about a mile east of the town, and was surrounded by a garden and a small orchard, where the apples were an irresistible temptation to boys, as he rather bitterly complained, especially as he was strangely proud of being a Justice of the Peace. His first wife received me, a woman who had evidently been very pretty, as indeed was shown by a portrait of her in youth that hung in the dining-room—pretty beyond question, proving that Hardy was easily overcome by beauty, as even Socrates used to say of himself. But perhaps she was not remarkable for power of intelligence. Gossip said she thought she had rather demeaned her caste by marrying the son of a shopkeeper, and the townspeople of Dorchester were inclined to make light of their famous man for the same reason. She was proud of being nearly related to an Archdeacon (one may remember that both Eustacia and Tess were proud of their birth and relationships). When the servant made some little mistake at tea, she said to me rather impatiently, "You see, Thomas always thinks every maid is a Tess!" And his natural sympathy for everyone of low estate very likely justified the irony.

As I had lately returned from Moscow after the Revolution that failed, Hardy talked chiefly about Russia, but presently he walked with me to the cottage home of the Dorset poet Barnes, whose works he had selected and edited, and whom he admired, though he thought his poems would often be improved by the omission of the last verse which dragged in a tag of morality in the mid-Victorian manner. He also thought there was too much of that kind of morality in Quiller-Couch's "Oxford Book of Verse"—a fault I had not noticed myself. On our way to Barnes's old church and Celtic monument, he told me that Louis Napoleon, afterwards called "Napoleon the Little", used to visit Came Park, in which the church stood, and nearly married one of the daughters there, which would certainly have altered European history. He talked freely about the characters in his books. He thought country people were becoming more like them rather than less, and the half-educated girl especially was now much like Tess, or Sue in "Jude" which he considered his greatest book, perhaps because it was his last and had been ruthlessly abused. Many girls of the same type wrote to him—small teachers, musicians, and milliners, some asking how they could contrive to live in the country.

He spoke a good deal, too, about sport, and said he had once really induced a sportsman not to go out shooting. And he told how the landowners in the neighbourhood had turned with indignation against him because in "Tess" he had described the agony of the wounded pheasants in their plantations. For a long time they refused to call on him.*

But Hardy was always moved to indignant pity for any animal suffering for man's pleasure or even man's necessity, and I recalled the letter he sent to *The Times* early in the Boer War, urging our commanding officers not to bring horses under fire—a vain appeal when all the enemy were mounted and tanks had not been invented. In the course of our walk he pointed to a distant cliff on which we could see the monument to Nelson's Hardy, and in the church he showed me a tablet to a Thomas Hardy of Elizabeth's reign. The family, he told me, came from Jersey, and his own grandfather used to sail to Ireland and from that country brought back an Irish wife, which perhaps introduced a "Celtic" strain into Hardy's own nature. He also pointed out the beginning of Egdon Heath, and other places described in his books.

He complained bitterly of a certain well-known critic who had said that Hardy's books would not live because they had no moral principle, and he added that the critic had not attempted to show that there was such a thing as a moral principle. He considered that the foundation of Ruskin College in Oxford was due to "Jude", but the Oxford dons were angry about the book, though they were getting over it now. People were always very stupid in taking dramatic sentences as representing his own opinions. But he had ceased to care much about his prose books, and, if he could have afforded it, he would have written nothing but verse. When a lyric was done, he said, it was something actual produced. One was never

---

* Much the same thing happened to John Masefield many years later when the sporting gentry were definitely frigid towards him after his condemnation of fox-hunting in "The Square Peg".

certain about prose, but you could get the whole of a novel into three pages of verse. To his love of verse he often returned. At the time he was much occupied with "The Dynasts", and he thought he was right in turning Parliamentary Debates into verse when the argument was high, as in one of Pitt's last speeches. He thought that neither side could ever be right in big controversies like that, but the English were on the whole less wrong than Napoleon. On the raging question of Home Rule, again, he was never very enthusiastic, but thought the Irish should have made the utmost of the English alliance so as to save their women and children from poverty. I was an extreme Sinn Feiner, but I would not bandy words with my King, as Johnson said of his difference with George III.

Next day we walked into Dorchester, and he showed me the shop that had been kept by the father of Sir Frederick Treves, the great surgeon, and the house where Judge Jeffreys lived during his Bloody Assize. Also the road to the village three miles out, where he himself was born. We cycled along the Weymouth road to the top of the Ridgeway, and walked out on the left to a farm beside the plantation giving a wide view over Weymouth and Portland (the Isle of Slingers), and far inland to nearly all the places mentioned in his books. The Start and St. Alban's Head were both mistily visible. Kipling had been much pleased with the place, and wanted to build a house there, and when Hardy told him all the windows would be shaken by the big guns firing off Portland, he said that would especially delight him. Hardy said he liked Kipling very much as a companion, and thought he would have been a very great writer if the Imperialists had not got hold of him. He also showed me the point in the road which the soldiers had reached when they heard that the rumour of Napoleon's landing was false. We climbed about the dykes and mounds of the ancient fortifications on "Maiden Castle", for he habitually lived in the past as in the present.

But to me more significant in the history of the man himself was our wandering in the town of Dorchester, where he showed me the railings he used to climb up as a boy to watch the hangman having his tea at a cottage in a hollow below on the evening before an execution, and wonder how the man could eat anything so soon before his terrible task. He told how the townspeople in the morning used to wait till the last moment on the chance of a reprieve. On an old map of the town he also pointed out to me a hardly distinguishable mark where the gallows had stood. More terrible yet was the spot in the midst of the Roman amphitheatre just south of the modern railway station, where a woman was burnt alive not long ago on suspicion of having poisoned her husband, which was the crime of "petty treason". She was known to have a lover, and they waited for six months till her baby was born, and then they burnt her alive in the midst of those ancient grassy slopes, on which the populace sat to see. Soon after my visit Hardy published a long account of the trial and execution in *The Times*, but I have not found the exact date.

Such subjects had for him the horrible fascination that comes of extreme sensitiveness to other people's agony. One finds repeated traces of it in "Tess" and "Jude" and many of the tales. If we all felt that sensitive sympathy and imagination, I suppose we should never cause pain to any living creature, certainly not for our pleasure or our pride. I remember the violent outbreak of rage among the peasants in South Russia when a party of English sportsmen went rook-shooting in

Thomas Hardy

their village, and the still more violent rage among Egyptian peasants when English officers went pigeon-shooting at Denshawai in the Nile Delta. That was an outburst of native violence and of vengeful English cruelty that marks a shameful page in our history (1906).*

Later on I was with Hardy two or three times, either in the flat he took near the Edgware Road or again at Max Gate, when he had his second wife with him, a woman of thoughtful beauty. When I was with him in the April of 1914, the air was full of rumours of war-omens and apprehension, and he showed me a poem he had just written for the *Fortnightly*, representing the dead as hearing the big guns of the new *Dreadnoughts*, and supposing them to sound the end of the world to be closely followed by the Last Judgment. During the terrible war which was so soon to follow I do not remember meeting him, though I had correspondence with him about a reprieve for my friend Roger Casement which he refused to sign. But after the war I was able to be with him again and witness a significant evidence of his retiring nature. On February 10, 1920, I was in Oxford, being sent by my great editor H. W. Massingham to write on a performance of "The Dynasts". I met the young poet Robert Nichols there, and he asked me to cross the Thames and its tributaries with him to Ferry Hinksey, where Sir Walter Raleigh had a beautiful house in which Hardy was staying. Masefield was also there, and the poet Robert Graves. Hardy received me very graciously, and regretted he saw me now so seldom. Mrs. Hardy, always so attractive in her thoughtful silence, welcomed me too, and in the evening we all met again in the New Theatre in George Street where

* See "Preface for Politicians" in Bernard Shaw's "John Bull's Other Island".

19

Thomas Hardy

"The Dynasts" was to be performed by the O.U.D.C. under Captain Colbourne as President.

There was a full house, the audience being made up chiefly of Undergraduates, Dons and their wives. The vast epic-drama had been very much abbreviated, as I had seen it once before played in London. It was well performed, and great applause rose at the end, with loud cries for "Author". Hardy himself was sitting beside me, and I several times urged him just to rise at all events, if not to appear on the stage. I told him that the young men and women there would in the far future glory in the memory that they had seen him in person at his great play. As the applause and calls continued, I turned to him with another appeal. But he was not there. He had stolen silently away into the street outside. I cannot doubt that he was inwardly pleased by such a reception, such a recognition of his genius after the long labour of the drama's composition and research. But he was gone. Like a shy animal he had crept away without a word, and I think I never saw him again.

I was present at his funeral service in Westminster Abbey— a service in which he would not have accepted a word as true to his reason, though he would have rejoiced in the ancient grandeur of the building and in the beauty of the language and music. Bernard Shaw, James Barrie, Arnold Bennett, Galsworthy, Belloc, A. E. Housman, E. M. Forster and Kipling were there, and for politics Stanley Baldwin and Ramsay MacDonald. But as I stood beside the hole into which his ashes were lowered, it was not of the music or the architecture or the distinguished mourners that I thought, but of that Egdon Heath which he had described in the first pages of "The Return of the Native":—

Men (he wrote) have oftener suffered from the mockery of

Thomas Hardy

a place too smiling for their reason than from the oppression of surroundings over-sadly tinged. Haggard Egdon appealed to a subtler and scarcer instinct, to a more recently learnt emotion, than that which responds to the sort of beauty called charming and fair.

The time seems near, if it has not actually arrived, when the chastened sublimity of a moor, a sea, or a mountain will be all of nature that is absolutely in keeping with the moods of the more thinking among mankind.

So we took our leave of that spirit of noble genius, chastened sublimity and a sadness deeply implanted in him by the pity of the world. That was on January 16, 1928, and the thirteen years that have passed up to 1941 would have brought little relief to the oppression of surroundings oversadly tinged. In *The Times* of January 11, 1928, was published a letter from Professor Albert Cock, telling us that when he was with Hardy at Max Gate in 1922, he expressed his gratitude for the note of deliverance offered in the last line of "The Dynasts", but Hardy shook his head and said—"I should not write that now". "Why not?" asked the Professor in surprise. Thomas Hardy replied, "Versailles". The great and deeply sympathetic poet foretold what now we see and suffer.

CHAPTER II

TELLER OF TALES

Once when Hardy was reading something I had written on him, he asked me not to call him a novelist. It was not that he would much rather have been known as a poet, but because, as he said, "Everyone is a novelist now". Certainly it is true that most popular writers are novelists. The novel is the modern form of art in words, just as the drama was the Elizabethan form. Among writers and readers it is commonly identified with "creative art", or even with "literature", though drama is sometimes coupled with it. Lyrical poetry, which implies beauty, has almost ceased to exist; for in its modern form, being without metre or rhyme, it has become an essay. It might just as well be printed as prose; and, though an essay, like one of Sir Thomas Browne's or Lamb's or Ruskin's, is sometimes "creative" in beauty of thought and sound, the wide distinction between prose and poetry will still be recognized by those who have ears to hear. Hardy at all events recognized that distinction very keenly, and so, though he was a "creative" writer, he objected to being called a novelist.

What, then, should we call him? It is as a novelist that he is most widely known. Perhaps "A Teller of Tales" would serve; for the majority of his works are tales or stories, and all mankind, from children and savages onward, love a story. Myths, mysteries, religions, superstitions, legends, fairy tales, histories, biographies, autobiographies, gossipings . . . all of them, whether exact or inexact, have taken the form of stories, and have widely retained their form because, like children, we do not like to have a story altered. Speaking for myself, I prefer other forms of literature to novels. To read a poor novel is the very cruellest way of slaughtering time. I should far rather sleep, or even play cards. But a great novel is too engrossing. I become one with the characters. I live in the scene. I am entangled in the plot. I am no longer myself, but transfigured. My own life ceases to have interest for me, and my private estimates of existence fade. The humorous or farcical passages in Dickens or Wodehouse lay an unreal glamour of charity and cheerfulness over the world, while profound tragedies like "Tess" and "Jude" shed, in Wordsworth's phrase, a melancholy over all my day. There I and sorrow sit.

Hardy wrote no farce, but he wrote humorous comedy, and above all he wrote tragedy. As Bernard Shaw divided his plays into "Pleasant" and "Unpleasant", so Hardy's novels might be divided into "Comparatively Cheerful" and "Profoundly Sad". Both kinds grew from his own nature, and his own nature grew from his own native earth and race. Some great writers, especially poets, have belonged to their own little group of stars, hills, valleys, or even streets, and they have failed when they turned from their homes. Burns lived Ayrshire, Wordsworth the Lakes; Scott lived Scotland, both High and Low, Lamb and Johnson lived London; Quiller-Couch, Cornwall; A. E. Housman, the Marches of Wales. Hardy lived the few central counties of southern England which he called Wessex, borrowing the name from the old Heptarchy. It is a land of characteristic English beauty, unnoticed by foreigners and unvisited by mountaineers and tourists in search of violent sports or "the picturesque": a land of low hills and dales, of streams clear and sometimes rapid, of many trees, copses and woods, beneath which lie depths of chalk deposited by long ages of ocean, and harder rock, perhaps smelted when earth was a fiery little star. Pastures and orchards grew on the surface, but in Hardy's youth wide spaces still were left untilled and open as moors and heaths, which he called by such names as Blackmoor Vale, Froom Vale, and the ominous Egdon Heath.* At the beginning of "The Return of the Native", he describes Egdon Heath or Waste minutely, and the scene pervades many of his own creations. He writes in a passage which I have already quoted in part:—

The spot was, indeed, a near relation of night, and when night showed itself, an apparent tendency to gravitate together could be perceived in its shades and the scene. . . . The qualifications which frequently invest the façade of a prison with far more dignity than is found in the façade of a palace double its size lent to this heath a sublimity in which spots renowned for beauty of the accepted kind are utterly wanting. . . .

In that description of the Heath the true nature of Hardy's works is more clearly seen than in any careful analysis of their powers and qualities. Egdon Heath, as he saw it, was the man himself, and the spirit of that Heath is felt in all the best that he wrote. Except in one or two of the early stories, such as "Under the Greenwood Tree", there is little to be called charming and fair, but we move in an atmosphere more sublime and subtle, like the shadows of night. We seem to be passing over a lonely moorland, swept by wind, rain and mist. Under our feet lie ancient crusts of Earth in which we may still discover the petrified relics of trilobites and other primeval

* Identification with the present-day names is aided by the list given in the Preface to the 1895 edition of "Tess of the D'Urbervilles".

forms of life. On one hand are earthen mounds heaped up to perpetuate the memory of long-forgotten kings: and not far off rise the gigantic rocks drawn by unknown means from far distant quarries and here set on end, or laid athwart as square arches, for the worship of some long-forgotten god. Not far away also broods the infinite sublimity of the sea, seldom here gleaming with innumerable smiles but usually grey or purple in gloom, revealing only a hazy distinction between the horizon and the clouds.

On such a scene Hardy was always conscious of "the dark backward and abysm of time". He saw the generations of man moving for centuries across those heaths and along the valleys, building their little shelters against cold and rain, scraping the soil for food, taming sheep and cattle for food and wool and hides, taming horses to double the human legs and strength, planting any imported fruit trees that could stand the British air, multiplying in families slowly like other higher animals, jealously contending for mates, begetting, bearing, being born and buried. Hardy was one of those who can live two lives in time and many lives in imagination beside his own. In the towns and villages of his Wessex he could become the small citizens and peasants—laborious, hard-living people, working for their lives along the course between birth and death, fairly honest in their dealings, shrewd and reticent, meaning more than they say, given to understate in irony, but taking pleasure in that abiding form of history which is gossip and slander, enjoying solid food and heavy drink, capable of shy laughter, speaking a fine form of abbreviated English, which retains many excellent words and phrases that, unhappily, have fallen out of use in other parts of our country.

But underneath all the humour, the interest in one another's lives, and the search for bodily pleasures, lay a shadow of something vaguely spiritual. It can be dimly traced in the frequent quotations from the English Bible, chiefly from the Old Testament stories, but often from the prophets; even so little read a poet as "holy Hosea", whom at the end of "Far from the Madding Crowd" Joseph Poorgrass quotes, "In my scripture manner, which is my second nature". But below these passages out of the Bible, familiar from their repetition in church, chapel and Sunday school, lie unwritten memories of far more ancient forms of religion—superstitions, as we call them, charms, and the omens which serve as indirect warnings from the natural world, such as the threefold crowing of a cock, the movements of slugs, toads and spiders. And there is a touch of the unearthly and devilish even about the dyed scarlet of the reddleman whenever he appears, as in that fine opening scene in "The Return of the Native". We see him red as Mephisto, gently driving his little cart across the gloomy Heath—gently because beloved Thomasin was sheltering in it. This action was praiseworthy, his nature was singularly trusty and honest; yet wherever he intruded, red as the devil, a half-conscious shudder passed through the people present. It was the inherited instinct of an ancient religion.

Among the natives of that remote and seldom visited part of our country there even existed a few whose thoughts and desires rose above the level of their farming and pastoral neighbours. Sometimes their higher degree of intelligence and hope or endeavour was the very cause of the tragedy which ultimately overwhelmed them. They belonged to what Walter Pater once called "The Aristocracy of Passion", and their passion reached beyond the desires that are common to nearly all human beings. Writing of Clym Yeobright ("Return of the Native"), Hardy tells us with irony but in truth:—

The rural world was not ripe for him. A man should be only partially before his time; to be completely to the vanward in aspirations is fatal to fame. . . . A well-proportioned mind is one which shows no particular bias; one of which we may safely say it will never cause its owner to be confined as a madman, tortured as a heretic, or crucified as a blasphemer. Also, on the other hand, that it will never cause him to be applauded as a prophet, revered as a priest, or exalted as a king. Its usual blessings are happiness and mediocrity.

The finest of Hardy's characters are not well-balanced. Of Clym Yeobright himself we read: "The only absolute certainty about him was that he could not stand still in the circumstances amid which he was born." Neither could Eustacia, in the same story, one of the very finest among the women. She was always longing for a full life, a life of stirring events, gaiety and vital companionship, such as she imagined Paris would naturally supply, or even Budmouth on some degree. Bathsheba ("Far from the Madding Crowd") we see first gazing at her own beauty in a mirror, and later on we are reminded of the local proverb that "Pride and vanity have ruined many a cobbler's dog". Yet it was not personal vanity that betrayed her to misfortune. It was her longing for actions brilliant and dashing like Sergeant Troy's sword-play—something removed from the commonplace of her surroundings, something finer and more unusual than the constancy and devotion of her lover Gabriel Oak, unusual as those virtues would be in any society. It was just because of this desire for something afar that Bathsheba becomes so lovable. But it was this, too, that brought her to that utter despair when she opened Fanny

Robin's coffin, and when for the revelation of his falsity her husband rejected her, being also overcome by his past love and remorse for the dead woman and their child.

And, indeed, Bathsheba was not the only victim to Sergeant Troy's dashing prowess. Of all the many scenes of pathos in Hardy's works, I think there is none more heartrending than the account in Chapter XL of Fanny Robin's struggle along the endless road to Casterbridge hospital when great with child by him. Next perhaps to two passages in "Tess" it stands highest as a record of natural love misplaced. It is some comfort in that fine story—the first that brought Hardy to high fame—that at the last Bathsheba and Gabriel Oak are joined in trustful love. It is some comfort, but one half suspects that this comforting consummation was perhaps devised to hold the favour of the sensitive English public, who, like Charles Darwin, "demand a happy ending".

In "Tess of the D'Urbervilles" no such attempt at comfort is made. Partly for that reason, but chiefly because the main subject treats of the passionate and hardly resistible attraction of a man's nature to a woman, even when the passion is not returned, the publishers were for some while unwilling to undertake the responsibility of putting their name to so poignant and natural a book. It appeared by instalment in various magazines, and was not united into a volume till 1891. In his Preface to later editions Hardy mentions other critics, among whom I like best "a gentleman who turned Christian for half-an-hour the better to express his grief that a disrespectful phrase about the Immortals should have been used". I suppose that brief convert was thinking of the last paragraph where Hardy wrote, "The President of the Immortals (in Æschylean phrase) had ended his sport with 'Tess'."

Thomas Hardy

That sport of the Immortals is revealed in the most tragic of all the tales. Step by step those pitiless hunters pursue a lovable and highly-tempered woman to so terrible a climax that I can still hardly endure to follow the infernal chase to the very end. It begins with the folly of her father Durbyfield and his silly claim to ancestral "family"; and one may notice that in many of the tales a sense of class distinction plays some part, probably because Hardy had himself been made conscious of it in his own family and town. By a careless accident Tess causes the death of the horse needed for the family's livelihood, and "thereafter she regarded herself in the light of a murderess", foreshadowing her doom like the irony of a Greek play. Unaware of danger, "for Nature does not often say 'See!'," she falls into the power of Alec D'Urberville, is struck with admiration of his headlong driving as Bathsheba was by Troy's sword-play. Then came the natural yielding of a passionate woman's nature to what is falsely called seduction. The sport of the Immortals was followed in bringing the higher nature into intimacy with a lower:—

Why so often the coarse appropriates the finer thus, the wrong man the woman, the wrong woman the man, many thousand years of analytical philosophy have failed to explain to our sense of order.

Step by step the Immortals continued their malignant sport —the baptism of the baby by Tess herself, without clerical rites, its death and burial, the revival of possible life and joy in her heart: "The irresistible, universal, automatic tendency to find sweet pleasure somewhere, which pervades all life, from the meanest to the highest, had at length mastered Tess." The next step in the pursuit was the renewed meeting with Angel Clare, their marriage, his confession of previous

29

error with a woman, her piteous confession to him of her previous error also, and his immediate rejection of her.

There is much in "Tess", as in most of Hardy's finest books, that is to myself incredible. That a young man just married to a beautiful and passionate woman who loved him with her whole being, alone in the night and beyond the reproach of scandal or law, should suddenly turn from her owing to a confession similar to his own, should turn from her beauty and thwart the natural desires of both—what kind of a chilly-blooded sea-monster must he have been? How could a human man tell her, "You were one person; now you are another. The woman I have been loving is not you; another woman in your shape." Hardy attempts apologies for the wretched creature:—

Some might risk the odd paradox that with more animalism he might have been the nobler man. We do not say it. Yet Clare's love was doubtless ethereal to a fault.

And later on we read:—

With all his attempted independence of judgment this advanced and well-meaning young man, a sample product of the last five-and-twenty years, was yet the slave to custom and conventionality when surprised back into his early teachings.

We must leave it at that, but it is no excuse for a bloodless nature. It is an unanswerable denunciation of that cruel convention under which the inhuman being had been nurtured in his parents' country vicarage. Ever onward, step by step, the Immortals pursued their chase—the departure of Angel Clare to Brazil, the rumour that he had offered to take Izz with him, the ruin of the Tess family, the appeal to Angel to return and save her from temptation, her marriage with

Thomas Hardy

D'Urberville as being her actual husband by seduction, Angel's too late return, Tess's overwhelming grief, the murder, the capture in Stonehenge (where a man worthy of love would have killed her on "The Stone of Sacrifice"), the visit to the prison, the black flag upon the tower. So the sport of the Immortals ended. It is a tragedy of a persistent and evil fate. Aristotle, "the master of those who know", tells us that the purpose of tragedy is to purge our emotions by means of pity and fear. But, in my case, the pity, far from purging my emotions of excess, remains so intolerable that, as I said, I can still hardly endure to read the final destruction of such a soul and body.

"Jude the Obscure", the last of Hardy's tales, began as a serial, and was published in full at the end of 1894. It was met with such a storm of hostile criticism that Hardy resolved to write no more prose but to concentrate upon verse and his epic drama. In the great but desperate work of "Jude", the Immortals pursued the main personality with two hounds, one the same as was used for Tess, the other of a slightly different breed. Hardy says in his preface that he here attempted to deal unaffectedly with the fret and fever, derision and disaster, that may press in the wake of the strongest passion known to humanity; to tell without mincing of words the deadly war waged with old Apostolic desperation between flesh and spirit; and also to paint the tragedy of unfulfilled aims. Both these hounds of the Immortals' sport become in Jude's case Hounds of Hell, though for some men they are fairly good and quiet. The Hound of natural desire for the continuance of life in the future race is the more inevitable and the more disastrous. It is he who, turning and twisting, hunts down Jude to the death. The other—his passionate desire for learning and an intellectual

31

life—might have been appeased but for the English insolence of class, and the contumely of Oxford dons towards a working man athirst for the learning they were paid to impart to wealthy young pleasure-seekers who cared nothing at all for it.

In the form of Arabella the power of sex, which is sometimes so gracious a blessing, runs through the whole book from her first deliberate seduction of a grave and artistic youth, to the deceit which compels him into marriage, then to a common and insensitive existence, as seen in the ? ? sticking episode; so to Jude's futile attempt at suicide, in imitation of his mother—an attempt followed by ineffective drunkenness. Arabella emigrates with her parents to Australia where she marries again, but, most unhappily, returns as Clare had returned in "Tess". Meantime, Jude's cousin Sue has appeared upon the scene. She is a wildly romantic and daring girl, at first pagan, then Anglican; she swims a river to escape from her Girls' Training School; she leaps from a window to escape the embrace of a husband whom "she could not stomach". There follow many complications, becoming more and more disastrous when Arabella sends to Jude a melancholic boy whom she declares to be his. He is called "Old Time", or "Time" for short, and in a fit of despair over the misery of the world—a despair inherited from his father and grandmother—he hangs himself and Sue's two babies on the back of the door—an appalling scene. Both Jude and Sue remarry their former spouses, in spite of a legal divorce on each side, and with resultant miseries to all four. Hardy has made a trifling mistake towards the end, where he makes the Oxford Eights coincide with the "Commemm.", but he then depicts a fine scene in which, deserted on his deathbed by all, Jude hears the shouting and applause rising from the Sports outside;

and as the cheering of the Oxford men continues, he whispers to himself the consummate lamentation of Job:—

Let the day perish wherein I was born, and the night in which it was said, there is a child conceived. . . . Why died I not from the womb? Why did I not give up the ghost when I came out of the belly? For now should I have lain still and been quiet. I should have slept: then had I been at rest. . . . Why is light given to him that is in misery, and life unto the bitter in soul?

He whispers nearly the whole of that superb passage. He lies stretched out alone on the lodging-house bed. Arabella, who had decked herself up for the Sports, was making love to the doctor as her next "chance". When she comes back and finds Jude dead as she expected, she remarks to another woman who is with her, "Yes. He's a 'andsome corpse". It is a tremendous story, full of pity and fear, whether it purges our emotions by means of them or not. When I first read it I thought it the greatest of Hardy's tales. Now it seems too horrible. The descriptions of the pig-sticking and of the half-crazy boy's hanging of himself and of the two babies on nails behind the door, are hardly endurable to me, though in a long experience as war-correspondent I have witnessed many horrible scenes. It was a sound rule of the old Roman poet and critic that Medea should not kill her children on the stage. Some imagined events cannot be borne when visible by sight and audible to hearing. Hardy's tenderly sensitive and melancholic nature, with feelings intensified by the pities and fears of his boyhood in Dorchester, perhaps led him to a breach in that long-established canon of art. To myself, at all events, the horror of such breaches reduces the worth of a story so subtle in discernment of character, and, on the practical side, so influential in effect. To many beside the Oxford Dons and Masters of Colleges it revealed the habitual shame of the privilege granted to wealth, while one of the "lower classes" who hungered and thirsted for wisdom was excluded from the chance of gaining it. While that exclusion remained unrelieved it was no wonder that to Jude, as to many of us Oxford men, it seemed impossible that modern thought could, in Hardy's words, "house itself in such decrepit and superseded chambers".

But apart from the creation of the characters and the perplexities involving them, the intention and purport of the book are not University reform or even the removal of our shameful inequalities of class and wealth. They are the more personal and intimate problems of love and marriage. These are suggested chiefly by Sue in various passages after her marriage with the generous but stiff and unattractive Phillotson, though in heart she loves only Jude throughout. They may be understood from a few quotations.

While Jude is still struggling with theology, she says to him:—

Some women's love of being loved is insatiable; and so, often, is their love of loving; and in the last case they may find that they can't give it continuously to the chamber-officer appointed by the bishop's licence to receive it.

A little later, when his belief in the Church's doctrines is beginning to totter, she leans to him from a window, just kisses his head, and says:—

When people of a later age look back upon the barbarous customs and superstitions of the times that we have the unhappiness to live in, what *will* they say?

Thomas Hardy

Again, she says to her husband, whom she likes but cannot love or allow to love her to the full:—

For a man and woman to live on intimate terms when one feels as I do is adultery, in any circumstances, however legal. There—I have said it!

In those sentences there is enough object for meditation among lovers, whether married or not, and there was enough cause to rouse a questioning and violent opposition to the book among the conventional, and even among the more thoughtful and dubious inquirers, at the end of last century.

As a final touch of Hardy's habitual irony, visible throughout his works, and to perfection concentrated in "Life's Little Ironies", I may quote the scene in which Jude and Sue are awaiting the coroner's verdict on the murder of her babies by Jude's despairing son:—

A subdued, large, low voice spread into the air of the room from behind the heavy walls at the back.

"What is it?" said Sue, her spasmodic breathing suspended. "The organ of the college chapel. The organist practising, I suppose. It's the anthem from the seventy-third psalm, 'Truly God is loving unto Israel.'"

She sobbed again. "O my babies! They had done no harm! Why should they have been taken away and not I!"

There was another stillness—broken at last by two persons in conversation somewhere without.

"They are talking about us, no doubt!" moaned Sue. "We are made a spectacle unto the world, and to angels, and to men!"

Jude listened—"No, they are not talking of us," he said. "They are two clergymen of different views, arguing about the eastward position."

The eastward position! Perhaps I was wrong in imagining

that every possible calamity had fallen upon Jude. In spite of his desire at one time for Ordination, he had escaped that.

It has been said, and I have been inclined to agree, that even in his finest stories Hardy sometimes causes the tragedy to arise from mere accidents and coincidences, as in "The Return of the Native". More serious, I think, is his repeated use of unexpected and disastrous "return", as in the return of Angel Clare in "Tess", and the return of Arabella in "Jude". But after all, both accident and return were used by the Greek tragedians. The accidental meeting of father and son at the cross-roads between Thebes and Delphi was the cause of the Œdipus tragedy; and the unexpected return of Agamemnon from Troy was the cause of the tragedy which has rightly been called the highest achievement of the human intellect.

CHAPTER III

THE POEMS

As I mentioned in the first chapter, Hardy told me he would not have written stories but for the necessity of making a livelihood. He would have written nothing but poems. Except in very rare cases, such as Tennyson's, poetry would certainly never win a livelihood in this country, but an inborn compulsion was always driving Hardy to compose it. I used to think his desire a mistake. I used to regard the necessity that impelled him to his prose stories as one of the blessings of adversity, but I understand now that it was impossible for his poetic nature to refrain from poetry. He saw men and nature and the situations of people to one another and to nature always from the poetic side. Instinctively he penetrated below obvious and superficial aspects into something deeper that could be revealed to him though not to all—something more deeply interfused, as Wordsworth said. Poetry is a revelation of the unseen, the unperceived, the unrecognized in common life. As Hobbes said of laughter, it is a sudden glory. It is in the power of the poetic mind to produce a sudden glory, a fresh joy, a revelation, even though the subject revealed may be sorrowful or tragic. And this poetic revelation may often be quick and complete.

In treating of any subject, poetry must also be the highest form of expression. Perhaps one should say the expression must be inseparably involved with the subject, just as in some beautiful or revolting personality the soul is indissolubly intermingled and expressed in the outward form, so that, after long experience of mankind, one may read in the whole body or even in face the exact index of soul. In its highest form, that is, I suppose, the poet's supreme power. It is a power of revelation, and it must be expressed in apt and suitably noble or beautiful language. To ensure the beauty of expression poets for many ages have spoken in metre, and for some centuries frequently in rhyme also. Metre and rhyme have been used partly for the pleasant or solemn sound, and partly, or perhaps chiefly, for memory. It is easier to recall words in metre than in prose, and the necessity of rhyme will often suggest to memory the corresponding line. As Goethe's Helena said, rhyme sounds as though the lines kissed each other. Hardy did not despise metre or rhyme.

As a poet he was disinclined to accept "Free Verse" as a good medium of poetic expression. Already a few years before his death the fashion of writing Free Verse was spreading, chiefly, I suppose, following the example of that noble-hearted and irresistible poet, Walt Whitman. In his ironic "Apology" for his second volume of verse (1922) Hardy apologized for quoting Tennyson "in the century of free verse". He may have recognized that the fashion was a revolt against the exquisite sweetness and rhythm of Tennyson and Swinburne. We have been witnessing a similar revolt in the arts of music, painting and sculpture. This is not the place for controversy on modes of poetry, but one may notice that so fine a critic as Horace, when expressing his admiration of Pindar and observing the difficulty of emulating him, says that he was borne on numbers released from rule (*numerisque fertur Lege solutis*)—in fact, wrote Free Verse. Yet great Greek scholars can trace a metre even in Pindar, and still more definitely in the Choruses of the Greek dramatists. Even Whitman is often not free from a kind of metre, and one might argue that many passages in our Authorised Translation of the Bible, as, for instance, in the Book of Job, Isaiah, and the Psalms, are in Free Verse. That true poet, Edward Thomas, once told me he thought Free Verse was not a poetic form because it was "too easy", and certainly we must accept the ancient Greek axiom that "The Beautiful is hard". But many acknowledged poets use Free Verse now, and my old friend Edward Carpenter, who possessed the poetic mind, laboured hard at the expression of his verse in imitation of his master Whitman, though his prose work was superior.

Hardy's metres are often strange, his sounds often harsh, his expression often crabbed. He has a way of introducing words that have become antiquated or were entirely local. He writes "Come weal, come *wanzing*", "*chasmal* beauty", " a lone cave's *stillicide*", "she *freshed*", "fear of death has even *bygone* us", and as though he were writing a telegram in which every word costs, "*unvision*", "*unweeting*", and "*unhope*" which is worse than William Morris's "wanhope". A "darkling thrush" may stand, since Keats borrowed the word from Milton as descriptive of a nightingale. But why, in the ten stanzas of a poem called "An Ancient to Ancients", he should in each stanza have repeated the word "Gentlemen" as a separate line I cannot understand. He is reviewing the great writers of the past, only to show how transitory is their fame as even Tennyson's has been:—

> The bower we shrined to Tennyson,
>   Gentlemen,
> Is roof-wrecked; damps there drip upon
> Sagged seats, the creeper nails are rust,
> The spider is sole denizen;
> Even he who voiced those rhymes is dust,
>   Gentlemen!

Thomas Hardy

Hardy's metre is far removed from the choice melody and verbal charm of Tennyson at his best, as he was in "The Lotos Eaters" and "In Memoriam". Hardy's metres are often harsh and uncouth; they fall at times into that "jingle" which Milton denounced—a denunciation which our "Modernists" have borrowed from that supreme poet without in the least acquiring his grandeur. It was against this uncouth harshness that George Meredith was protesting when he once said to me, "Yes, Hardy is a true master of prose, but I have no use for his verse". Yet at times how strong the metre is, how exactly suited to the theme, as in that terrible tale called "A Trampwoman's Tragedy", beginning—

> From Wynyard's Gap the livelong day,
>   The livelong day,
> We beat afoot the northward way
>   We had travelled times before.
> The sun-blaze burning on our backs,
> Our shoulders sticking to our packs,
> By fosseway, fields, and turnpike tracks
>   We skirted sad Sedgemoor.

That manner of repeating part of the first line in the second is here impressive, and perhaps original to Hardy, though Burns uses a repetition in the fifth line of each verse of "Annie Laurie". Hardy evidently liked it, for he used it again in "Great Things" and "He never expected much", that characteristic "Reflection", on his eighty-sixth birthday, and in "Song of the Soldiers' Wives".

Turning to the substance or purpose of the varied expressions, we find that in his first collection (1901) he divided them, like Wordsworth, into groups—*War Poems*, referring to the South African War of 1899 and the following two years;

Thomas Hardy

Poems of Pilgrimage, on various Continental scenes; a long collection of *Miscellaneous Poems*, mainly lyrics; *Imitations*, from classic and Continental lyrics; and *Retrospect*. In the volume of 1922 there are no divisions or groupings according to subject. The poems follow one another without any special order, though they are sometimes dated.

It is hard to make a general appreciation or estimate of lyrics so numerous and so varied in substance. Some are directly personal, dwelling upon his own life; memories of past love, or days of brief happiness, or the sense of neglected opportunities; or the knowledge that others are rising to fame and his name will soon be forgotten, as in "The Superseded":—

> 'Tis not that we have unforetold
> The drop behind;
> We feel the new must oust the old
> In every kind;
> But yet we think, must we, must we,
> Too drop behind?

Or the lamentation common to all ageing men who still feel young, the lamentation expressed with poignant brevity by Oscar Wilde when he said, "The worst of old age is not that we are old, but that we are young". So Hardy in "I Look into my Glass":—

> I look into my glass,
> And view my wasting skin,
> And say, "Would God it came to pass
> My heart had shrunk as thin!"
>
> For then, I undistresst
> By hearts grown cold to me,
> Could lonely wait my endless rest
> With equanimity.

Thomas Hardy

But Time, to make me grieve,
Part steals, lets part abide;
And shakes this fragile frame at eve
With throbbings of noontide.

His personality lies partly revealed in nearly all that Hardy
wrote, but only a few of his poems are definitely personal and
concern himself alone. His own epitaph runs thus:—

I never cared for Life: Life cared for me,
And hence I owe it some fidelity.
It now says, "Cease; at length thou hast learnt to grind
Sufficient toil for an unwilling mind,
And I dismiss thee—not without regard
That thou didst ask no ill-advised reward,
Nor sought in me much more than thou couldst find."

It is a suitable epitaph for a man so patient, and outwardly so
indifferent to criticism, though inwardly painfully sensitive
to it. But for a finer epitaph I should choose his poem called
"Afterwards":—

When the present has latched its postern behind my tremulous
stay,
And the May month flaps its glad green leaves like wings,
Delicate-filmed as new-spun silk, will the neighbours say,
"He was a man who used to notice such things?"

If it be in the dusk when, like an eyelid's soundless blink,
The dewfall-hawk comes crossing the shades to alight
Upon the wind-warped upland thorn, a gazer may think,
"To him this must have been a familiar sight."

If I pass during some nocturnal blackness, mothy and warm,
When the hedgehog travels furtively over the lawn,
One may say, "He strove that such innocent creatures should
come to no harm,
But he could do little for them; and now he is gone."

Thomas Hardy

If, when hearing that I have been stilled at last, they stand at
    the door,
Watching the full-starred heavens that winter sees,
Will this thought rise on those who will meet my face no more,
"He was one who had an eye for such mysteries"?

And will any say when my bell of quittance is heard in the
    gloom,
And a crossing breeze cuts a pause in its out-rollings,
Till they rise again, as they were a new bell's boom,
"He hears it not now, but used to notice such things"?

"Dewfall-hawk"? Perhaps nightjar.

There is the inner truth of the poet. He used to notice
such things. To him it was a familiar sight. He could do
little for innocent creatures, but he strove to do something.
He had an eye for such mysteries as the starry heavens.

Hardy's poetic personality tinged all his poems, but as a
rule he contrived to escape from self. In an essay upon Wordsworth's "Prelude", Lord Grey, after quoting the lines envying
a child's delight in the stories of Jack-the-Giant-killer and
Robin Hood, and the conclusion,

    The child whose love is here, at least, doth reap
    One precious gain, that he forgets himself,

goes on to speak of the loss suffered by men of great powers
in great place who were unable to forget themselves. "The
greater a man's powers, the more difficult it is for him to
forget himself".* Hardy, like Wordsworth, certainly felt that
difficulty. Wordsworth solved it by looking outside and finding
himself in sensitive sympathy with the joys and sorrows of
other men and women, until, speaking of the girl in "The Pet

* "Fallodon Papers", page 169.

Thomas Hardy

Lamb", he could say, "I almost received her heart into my own". So it was in many of his finest poems, such as "Lucy Gray", "The Reverie of Poor Susan", "The Leech-gatherer", "Michael", "The Solitary Reaper", in the Sonnets for England, and in so many others in which one hears the still, sad music of humanity. The beauty, the terror, the mysteries of nature and the Universe, also enabled him to escape from self. So it often happened with Hardy. He would take some event or situation or even some place, and by revealing its inner meaning would also unwittingly reveal himself. This might be in its tragedy, its irony, less often its joy or cheerfulness. Irony predominates, as in "The Ruined Maid", "Her late Husband", "One Ralph Blossom soliloquizes" (on seven maids he had seduced), "Royal Sponsors", "The Contretemps", "His Immortality", "The Conformers", "The Curate's Kindness (A Workhouse Irony)". Some of the poems are tragically pathetic, such as "The Chapel Organist" and "The Trampwoman's Tragedy". But to myself, especially revealing are observations of unmarked thoughts, such as "In the British Museum" (where a countryman, being told a block of stone came from the Areopagus, reflected that it had once heard St. Paul), or a thought of rare beauty, "Shelley's Skylark: (The Neighbourhood of Leghorn; March, 1887)", beginning,

> Somewhere afield here something lies
> In Earth's oblivious eyeless trust
> That moved a poet to prophecies—
> A pinch of unseen, unguarded dust:
>
> The dust of the lark that Shelley heard
> And made immortal through times to be;—
> Though it only lived like another bird,
> And knew not its immortality.

Lived its meek life; then, one day, fell—
A little ball of feather and bone;
And how it perished, when piped farewell,
And where it wastes are alike unknown.

.　.　.　.　.

Go find it, faeries, go and find
That tiny pinch of priceless dust,
And bring a casket silver-lined,
And framed of gold that gems encrust.

There are two other verses. The poem is an instance of a revealed thought that might escape any but the poet's mind.

Most of the poems end in sorrow—the sorrow's crown of sorrow remembering happier things, the sorrow of frustrated aims, the sorrow of the grave and the end of living, of questionings to the Universe and to God, who has indeed forgotten the wretched little earth and Man, as in "New Year's Eve" and "God-forgotten", in which God speaks:—

". . . And it is strange . . . though sad enough . . .
　Earth's race should think that one whose call
Frames daily shining spheres of flawless stuff
　Must heed their tainted ball! . . .

But say'st it is by pangs distraught,
　And strife and silent suffering? . . .
Sore grieved am I that injury be wrought
　Even on so poor a thing!"

As coming under the strong influence, not only of Darwin proclaimed in the middle of last century, but also of Schopenhauer and Hartmann, Hardy was naturally denounced as a

45

"pessimist". In reading such a poem as "In Tenebris" (1895),
it is hard to avoid the word:—

> Wintertime nighs;
> But my bereavement-pain
> It cannot bring again:
> Twice no one dies.
>
> Leaves freeze to dun;
> But friends can not turn cold
> This season as of old
> For him with none.
>
> Tempests may scath;
> But love cannot make smart
> Again this year his heart
> Who no heart hath.
>
> Black is night's cope;
> But death will not appal
> One who, past doubtings all,
> Waits in unhope.

This charge of pessimism moved Hardy to personal indignation.
The "Apology", which serves as Preface to the "Late Lyrics
and Earlier" (1922), is a strong protest:—

What is to-day, in allusions to the present author's pages,
alleged to be "pessimism" is, in truth, only such "questionings"
in the exploration of reality, and is the first step towards the
soul's betterment, and the body's also.

A forward conjecture scarcely permits the hope of a better
time, unless men's tendencies should change. Whether owing
to the barbarizing of taste in the younger minds by the stark
madness of the late war, the unabashed cultivation of selfish-
ness in all classes, the plethoric growth of knowledge simul-
taneously with the stunting of wisdom, "a degrading thirst

after outrageous stimulation" (to quote Wordsworth again), or from any other cause, we seem threatened with a new Dark Age.

After denouncing the negligent or ignorant criticisms, "which may have stifled a few true poets in the run of generations, but are dispersed like stricken leaves before the wind of next week, and are no more heard of again in the region of letters than their writers themselves", the writer continues in a calmer but still far from hopeful tone:—

In any event, poetry, pure literature in general, religion— I include religion, because poetry and religion touch each other, or rather modulate into each other; are, indeed, often but different names for the same thing—these, I say, the visible signs of mental and emotional life, must, like all other things, keep moving, becoming; even though at present, when belief in witches of Endor is displacing the Darwinian theory and "the truth that shall make you free", men's minds appear, as above noted, to be moving backwards rather than on.

Quoting from his own poem "In Tenebris", he urges, "If way to the Better there be, it exacts a full look at the Worst," but as some possible mitigation of the Worst he looks down the future ages and conjectures that whether the human and kindred animal races survive till the exhaustion or destruction of the globe, or whether these races perish and are succeeded by others before that conclusion comes, pain to all upon it, tongued or dumb, shall be kept down to a minimum by loving-kindness, operating through scientific knowledge.

Lovingkindness! In 1941, during the second of the two most destructive wars in history, that hope does not seem to be growing well, though we have plenty of scientific knowledge, chiefly employed to multiply destruction. Still, that Hardy should thus mention it, gives to his work a glimmer of pale hopefulness.

For his penetrating sympathy with external nature and with all living things Hardy will naturally be compared with Wordsworth, and we may turn again to what Lord Grey said of Wordsworth in that essay on "The Prelude". After the poet wrote that he had "yielded up all moral questions in despair", Lord Grey says, "He does not sit down under that despair":—

Whatever depression he goes through, he never ends the poem until he has found the thought which sets him on his feet, upright above depression. However great the depression, and it was at times as great as ever poet had, he never rests until he has found the point of view and the thought in which he can be strong again; where, instead of being a pessimist, he can be hopeful, sanguine, certain as regards the future.*

One cannot say that of Hardy. His hope was too like despair. People nowadays frequently accuse the Victorians of complacency, but I cannot understand why. The years that followed Wordsworth's death in 1850 were years of violent upheaval, of mental and social revolution, of moral uncertainty and of rebellion, aiming at the overthrow of much that had been thought essential in religion. The whole aspect of man's position in the Universe was suddenly changed and reversed. War succeeded war, and the wars were terrible and unjust. Far from being complacent, the Victorian Age and the following years up to Hardy's death might rather be called bewildering and desperate. Even the Russian revolutions, upon which we built high hopes, produced men who, in Wordsworth's own lines upon the French Revolution, "plucked up mercy by

* "Fallodon Papers," p. 175.

the roots", or in the earlier poet's words, "shut the gates of mercy on mankind". To a man of Hardy's insight and sensitive susceptibility such was the age through which he had to live, and only the blind and spiritually numb could endure such an age with complacency.

It was an age of great thought and great literature. One has only to remember the names of Carlyle, Ruskin, Dickens, Tolstoy, Victor Hugo, Mazzini, Swinburne, Marx, and many more—a flight of loudly crying and ominous birds—to realize that those were years of turbulence in all Europe's mental and social conditions. Of our chief English poets, Browning alone maintained a resolute optimism. But even his resolution sometimes appears rather forced, and there is nothing more depressing than deliberate optimism and self-willed belief. In such an age it was no wonder that Hardy, born rather frail and unfitted for boisterous enjoyment, associated from childhood with scenes and stories of murder and execution, knowing well the sorrows of the destitute, and feeling his profound religious instincts shaken by new and scientific questionings, should have been affected throughout with a sense of melancholy as he looked upon such a world and found so little in his own nature or in his surroundings to combat the temptations of despair. Schopenhauer, pessimism's apostle, discovered that pity is the ultimate distinction and virtue of mankind. In much the same manner, Hardy found that distinction and virtue in sympathy with all that breathes, and in lovingkindness among men of goodwill. In this year, nineteen-hundred-and-forty-one after Christ, even that way of salvation looks narrow and uncertain. For as I write, all the most intelligent races of mankind are killing one another as fast as they can, and at the same time by amazingly scientific means destroying the finest memorials of art and the most ingenious contrivances for fulness of life.

In these hideous times of murder and ruin it may well seem that Bertrand Russell was scientifically right in saying, "It is on the firm foundation of unyielding despair that the soul's habitation henceforth alone can be safely built". In the *Prologue to Faust*, Mephisto tells the Lord that the accursed race of Man goes on and is as ridiculous as on the First of Days. "A little better they might live, hadst Thou not given them the gleam of heaven's light. They call it Reason and use it only to live more beastly than the beasts." It is all true. The slaughter and ruin that men have brought upon each other is ridiculous or astonishing (*wunderlich*). From age to age murder and ruin have ensanguined and blackened the whole course of history and the present age is hardly worse than many in the past. Yet the accursed race goes on. Its numbers are estimated to be increasing, and even the surpassing allurements of love and procreation would hardly induce the majority of men and women to continue the increase if they realized that the only firm foundation for the soul were unyielding despair.

CHAPTER IV

"THE DYNASTS"*

Hardy is famous for his stories of Wessex. Four or five of them are imaginative works of great power and insight. To many besides poets he is known for his verse. But in my opinion "The Dynasts" is his masterpiece. He calls it an Epic Drama. It is certainly in dramatic form, for the characters— a vast number—speak in person, and it is divided into Parts and Acts and Scenes, a prose description of the places serving as background. In dramatized and much abbreviated form, chiefly representing Trafalgar and Waterloo, it has been produced on the stage in London, and, as before mentioned, I have seen it in Oxford, with Hardy himself seated beside me. But in spite of the dramatic form I should rather call it an epic.

Success in the Epic is a rare kind of success, and hardly half-a-dozen epics have stood the test of time. Hardy's theme differs from the others in one main aspect. The *Iliad* was founded on legends and mythology in which the poet seems almost to have believed as true. The *Æneid* was founded on similar legends and mythology of which the poet believed scarcely any. The *Divine Comedy* told of an infernal and celestial journey among people who once had existence but who no longer act as epic characters. The *Faëry Queen* shows us scenes of imaginary characters or abstract qualities. *Paradise Lost* was founded upon legends and mythology that the poet perhaps partially believed but which the knowledge of later times has made more in-

* Hardy pronounced the word "Dynasts" on the analogy of "dynamite" and "dynamic", ignoring the Greek short quantity.

credible than the works of the Greek or Roman or Italian. But Hardy dealt with actual history—a period of ten years well known to all educated English readers, and to be verified by documents upon which he laboured with minute accuracy, and the labour took him nearly seven years. He had to follow definite history instead of alluring legend, and to transform actual records into epic and drama. He could no longer use mythological figures of the same kind as the good or evil beings in Homer, Virgil, Dante or Milton.

In place of Gods, Goddesses, and Satans he introduced "impersonated abstractions or Intelligences, called Spirits" (whose words are always printed in italics). In the Preface he tells us:—

They are intended to be taken by the reader, for what they may be worth, as contrivances of the fancy merely. Their doctrines are but tentative, and are advanced with little eye to a systematized philosophy warranted to lift the burden of "the mystery of this unintelligible world" . . . These phantasmal Intelligences are divided into groups, of which one only, that of the Pities, approximates to the Universal Sympathy of human nature—the "spectator idealized" of the Greek Chorus; it is impressionable and inconsistent in its views, which sway hither and thither as wrought on by events.

After mentioning another group as the "Passionless Insight of the Age", Hardy proceeds with his explanation:—

In point of literary form, the scheme of contrasted Choruses and other conventions of this external feature was shaped with a single view to the modern expression of a modern outlook, and in frank divergence from classical and other dramatic precedent which ruled the ancient voicings of ancient themes.

Of the other Spirits "The Ancient Spirit of the Years" is but the stream of the Universe, flowing we know not whence or whither. "The Spirits Sinister and Ironic" are but our own dark or scornful thoughts, or such as spirits might think when watching the peculiar goings-on of mankind. "The Spirit of Rumour" we might call "The News"; "The Recording Angels", the Documents of History. But behind all these abstractions lies a further abstraction which the poet calls "The Immanent Will", or "Fundamental Energy", which, I suppose, expresses something the same idea as Schopenhauer's "*Wille*" or Bergson's "*Élan Vital*". Of this Immanent Will the Spirit of the Pities at once asks:—

> "Why doth it so and so, and ever so,
> This viewless, voiceless Turner of the Wheel?"

It seems impossible for the poet to make definite answer. He tells us, "The abandonment of the masculine pronoun in allusion to the First or Fundamental Energy seemed a necessary and logical consequence of the long abandonment by thinkers of the anthropomorphic conception of the same". At times during the dramatic poem this Immanent Will becomes almost visible. On the terrific field of Austerlitz we read:—

The Controlling Immanent Will appears therein as a brain-like network of currents and ejections, twitching, interpenetrating, entangling and thrusting hither and thither the human forms.

After the scene of Napoleon's coronation in Act I, we read:—

The scene assumes the prenatural transparency before mentioned, and there is again beheld as it were the interior of a brain which seems to manifest the volitions of a Universal Will, of whose tissues the personages of the action form portion.

At the beginning of the advance towards Moscow:—

Thomas Hardy

The unnatural light before seen usurps that of the sun, bringing into view, like breezes made visible, the films or brain-tissues of the Immanent Will, that pervade all things, ramifying through the whole army, Napoleon included, and moving them to Its inexplicable artistries.

Except for that Immanent Will, perhaps without thought, perhaps without purpose, there is no hint of Divinity. The three great Greek tragedians still retained some faith in Divine Powers, but "The Dynasts" is as devoid of personal Divinity as is Lucretius, perhaps even more devoid, for Lucretius at least symbolizes the goddess of procreation, the delight of gods and men. I doubt if it would be any consolation to a naturally religious mind to contemplate the Immanent Will as a brainlike network of currents and ejections, twitching, interpenetrating, entangling, and thrusting hither and thither the human forms. The Universe as we know it is but part, perhaps the whole, of that inexplicable Will, and we can attribute to it no quality, and not even a sense of time or space, though to ourselves events appear to follow each other within certain limits, as on a modern film. Under the influence of the Will, the phenomena that we call History appear to move and writhe, and in this stupendous drama we may watch them in succession moving and writhing as controlled by Time and Space. Perhaps also by Cause.

As through a long telescope, or powerful microscope that diminishes instead of magnifying, we are shown the hosts of conquerors, the doom of kings, the swarming populations of Europe on their passage through life during the early ten years of last century. Little figures run about; they love and hate, they suffer pain, they laugh and scream, they make a fine to-do over their pleasures and miseries. Here in white uniforms creeps the Austrian army, "with a movement as of molluscs on a leaf". We listen to William Pitt after the brief truce that followed the first war, telling the House of Commons the necessity of a second:—

> The preparations of the enemy,
> Doggedly bent to desolate our land,
> Advance with a sustained activity.
> They are seen, they are known, by you and by us all.

And a little later at the Guildhall, we hear him utter his famous words:—

> My lords and gentlemen—You have toasted me
> As one who has saved England and her cause.
> I thank you, gentlemen, unfeignedly.
> But—no man has saved England, let me say:
> England has saved herself, by her exertions:
> She will, I trust, save Europe by her example.

After Austerlitz we hear him say in his extreme illness, "Roll up the map. 'Twill not be needed now These ten years!" And then, his dying words: "My country! How I leave my country!" It all sounds lifelike, and yet reduced as though a living puppet spoke in a whisper. But none the less it is real, as was Sir Edward Grey's speech to the Commons in the fateful August of 1914. As on a diminished film there sails Nelson with his ships, the passionate love in his heart, and the scene in the cockpit of the *Victory* still before him. And there Napoleon, the protagonist of the prolonged tragedy, speeds from victory to victory, stamping great Empires down, lording it like a Dictator over Europe till in succession Trafalgar and Waterloo, as in a Greek tragedy, fall in vengeance upon his overweening pride. We see his return from Elba, his welcome by the devoted soldiers of his former triumphs

—one of the finest scenes of personal drama in all history—and so we come to a most minute and carefully elaborated description of Waterloo.

The steps both up and down on which the tragedy of Napoleon's fate moves under the compulsion of the Immanent Will are described with an historical accuracy due to Hardy's long and patient research. The account of his victory over the old Prussian army at Jena-Auerstadt, which I have followed carefully on the actual site, is exact in every point, except that Hardy does not give enough weight to the conclusive stroke of Davout's unexpected assault upon the left rear of the Prussian main force. Austerlitz, Wagram, Talavera, Albuera, Borodino, Leipzig, and Waterloo are described with an accuracy which proves a military genius subsisting in the brain of the Wessex poet. As descriptions of War's inevitable abominations I should choose three events in the murderous campaigns. It is hard to avoid a comparison between the failure at Walcheren and our Dardanelles campaign in 1915, though that gallant and well-designed attempt upon Constantinople at least kept the main Turkish armies bound to the narrow peninsula. Of Walcheren Hardy writes:—

A marshy island at the mouth of the Scheldt. . . . Sour grasses grow in places, and strange fishy smells, now warm, now cold, pass along. Brass-hued and opalescent bubbles, compounded of many gases, rise where passing feet have trodden the damper spots. . . . A vast army is encamped here, and in the open spaces are infantry on parade—skeletoned men, some flushed, some shivering, who are kept moving because it is dangerous to stand still. . . . In the distance soldiers are digging graves for the funerals which are to take place after dark, delayed till then that the sight of so many may not drive the living melancholy mad.

Secondly, on the retreat to Coruña: the season is the beginning of January and the country is covered with a sticky snow. In the gloom of a cellar in a deserted house are heaps of damp straw, in which ragged figures are lying half-buried, many of the men in the uniform of English line regiments, and the women and children in clouts of all descriptions, some being nearly naked. Most of the inmates are drunk (they had discovered barrels of wine hidden in the cellar):—

Fourth Deserter (*to a woman lying beside him*). "What d'ye think of that, my honey? It fairly makes me a man again. Come, wake up! We must be getting along somehow." (*He regards the woman more closely*) "Why my little chick? Look here, friends." (*They look and the woman is found to be dead.*) "If I didn't think her poor knees felt cold! And only an hour ago I swore I'd marry her!"

Before Coruña itself, a pathetic 14,000 of foot only is just deploying into line. The harassed force now appears as if composed of quite other than the men observed in the retreat insubordinately straggling along like vagabonds. Yet they are the same men, suddenly stiffened and grown amenable to discipline by the satisfaction of standing to the enemy at last. The French have an ominous superiority, both in position and in their abundance of cavalry and artillery:—

It is now getting on for two o'clock, and a stir of activity has lately been noticed along the French front. Three columns are descending from their position. . . . A clash ensues, the English being swept down in swathes by the enemy's artillery. The opponents meet face to face at the village in the valley between them, and the fight there grows furious. Sir John Moore is seen galloping to the front under a gloomy sky.

Again, on the appalling retreat of the French from Moscow, of which we have contemporary accounts by Berthier (in his

Thomas Hardy

letter to Napoleon, November 9, 1815) and other French
officers who shared it after Napoleon has escaped for Paris:—*

The stricken shadows in a limbo of gloom are among the
last survivors of the French army. Few of them carry arms.
. . . With their swords they cut rashers from a dead horse
and grill them in the flames, using gunpowder for salt to eat
them with. Two others return from a search, with a dead rat
and some candle-ends. . . . In the background enter some light
horse of the Russian army, followed by Kutuzof himself and
a few of his staff. . . . The whole detachment pauses at the
sight of the French asleep. They shout, but the bivouacs give
no sign.

KUTUZOF. "Go, stir them up! We slay not sleeping men."
    The Russians advance and prod the French with their lances.
RUSSIAN OFFICER. Prince, here is a curious picture. They
      are dead."
KUTUZOF (*with indifference*).
    "Oh, naturally. After the snow was down,
    I marked a sharpening of the air last night.
    We shall be stumbling on such frost-baked meats
    Most of the way to Wilna."
OFFICER (*examining the bodies*).   "They all sit
    As they were living still, but stiff as horns;
    And even the colour has not left their cheeks,
    Whereon the tears remain in strings of ice—
    It was a marvel they were not consumed;
    Their clothes are cindered by the fire in front,
    While at their back the frost has caked them hard."
KUTUZOF. "'Tis well. So perish Russia's enemies."†

And for what purpose or motive was all this intolerable

---

* For condemnation of Napoleon's callous abandonment of his
suffering army, see Tolstoy's "War and Peace", Part XIV, chapter 18.
  † For similar ghastly effects of cold see *The Times* Correspondent's
account of the suffering in Albania (*The Times*, January 6, 1941).

Thomas Hardy

suffering imposed upon the nations of Europe? We must take
the title of the Epic-Drama as Hardy's answer. To Prussia,
Russia, Austria, and Spain we are to suppose it was mainly a
question of Dynasty. I cannot think there was much of that
question in England. For even when the simple-minded
George III had ceased his innocent pleasures at Weymouth
and had to be confined in a padded room, there was not much
doubt as to the Prince Regent's succession, though his ex-
travagances, debauchery, uncertain marriage, and his shameful
treatment of his legal Queen, diminished the Royal popularity
among a people gradually returning to a Puritanic form of
religion and behaviour.

But in regard to Napoleon himself, the poet leaves us in
no doubt. In his first scene with childless Josephine, when all
had been conquered except England, his "sole enemy", and
Wellesley was draining the French resources in Spain, Napoleon
observes to the anguished Empress: "There is, of course, that
worm Time ever keeps in hand for gnawing me! The question
of my dynasty." Josephine was forty-three, and he charged her
with sterility. He was meditating divorce, with an eye fixed
on Marie Louise of Austria, and hoping to gain her through
the mediation of Metternich. At a masque ball soon after the
British collapse at Walcheren, he says to Madame Metternich:
"Children are needful to my dynasty, and if one woman cannot
mould them for me, why, then, another must." When he was
already at Charleroi, the night before Waterloo, a vision
passed through his brain as he slept, "comprising hundreds of
thousands of skeletons and corpses in various stages of decay.
They rise from his various battlefields, the flesh dropping
from them, and gaze reproachfully at him. His intimate
officers who have been slain he recognizes among the crowd."

A similar vision falls upon him just while Ney is charging on the field:—

> A horrible dream has gripped me—horrible!
> I saw before me Lannes—just as he looked
> That day at Aspern: mutilated, bleeding!
> "What—blood again?" he said to me. "Still blood?"

These visions seem to me hardly in place within the drama. They are too much like that picture in an old gallery in Brussels—a vision of multitudinous mothers holding up their slaughtered children to Napoleon's face in passionate reproach.

But, in any case, such considerations had no effect upon the Man of Destiny, nor had the sufferings and deaths of common animals (a characteristic touch in Hardy)—the coneys, moles, larks, hedgehogs, snails, and worms tormented by the thunder of guns and the charges of horse and foot. To the last his dream of Dynasty persists. After the chaotic flight from Waterloo the Spirit of the Years observes:—

> "So hath the urging Immanence used to-day
> Its inadvertent might to field this fray;
> And Europe's wormy dynasties rerobe
> Themselves in their old gilt, to dazzle anew the globe!"

And in his final speech, Napoleon says:—

> "If but a Kremlin cannon-shot had met me
> My greatness would have stood; I should have scored
> A vast repute, scarce paralleled in time.
>
> .   .   .   .   .
>
> Yes, a good death to have died on yonder field;
> But never a ball came passing down my way!
> So, as it is, a miss-mark they will dub me;
> And yet—I found the Crown of France in the mire,
> And with the point of my prevailing sword
> I picked it up! But for all this and this
> I shall be nothing. . . .

Thomas Hardy

> My only course
> To make good showance to posterity
> Was to implant my line upon the throne.
> And how shape that, if now extinction nears?
> Great men are meteors that consume themselves
> To light the earth. This is my burnt-out hour."

The longing to continue one's blood and name is common. We see it frequently among families of great power and possessions, as among those who were till lately the great landowners of England. We remember how "the heir" used to be acclaimed at birth and fêted at twenty-one. To maintain or create a family name seems to ensure a kind of vicarious immortality. Napoleon claimed to have had a son by Madame Walewska, the beautiful Pole; and the son of Marie Louise —Napoleon II, that unhappy boy who as "L'Aiglon" wore out his life at his mother's Court in Vienna—was also recognized as his son. To found a dynasty seemed a great purpose, but the underlying purpose even of a dynasty was to secure his own immortal fame—"a vast repute, scarce paralleled in time". In that last speech he mentions with envy those whose fame had been magnified by death in action—Nelson, Harold, Hector, Cyrus, Saul—heroic names; and he might have added Philip Sydney and Wolfe. Regretting the failure of his attempted suicide at Fontainebleau, he cried:—

> "Had I then ceased,
> This deep had been unplumbed; had they but worked" (the
>   poison drops he then tried)
> "I had thrown threefold the glow of Hannibal
> Down history's dusky lanes."

He need not thus have lamented. In Sir Thomas Browne's "Urn Burial" we are told that "Diuturnity is a dream and folly

61

of expectation", but until mankind's history is rolled up and laid aside by the Immanent Will, Napoleon's name will be inscribed upon it, and the long-drawn misery of his years in exile will be recorded as no less a tragedy than death upon the field.

Underneath all this tragic story of consuming ambition for perpetual fame, underneath the overthrow of dynasties and the thunder and shoutings of victories and defeats, the uncounted millions of usual men and women went on from day to day with life in millions of variations. As through the reverse end of that diminishing microscope, we are shown tiny villagers creeping about upon their daily business of food and warmth. They scramble up the little ant-heaps called hills. They listen to rumours and criticize gossip. They are amazed to see a real match struck upon tinder. They wonder if "Boney" will actually invade. Terrible stories go round about the Corsican Monster:—

WOMAN (*in undertones*). "I can tell you a word or two on't. It is about His victuals. They say that He lives upon human flesh, and has rashers of baby every morning for breakfast —for all the world like the Cernel Giant in old ancient times!"

YOUNG MAN. "Ye can't believe all ye hear."

PRIVATE. "I only believe half. And I only own—such is my challengeful character—that perhaps He do eat pagan infants when He's in the desert. But not Christian ones at home. Oh, no—'tis too much."

WOMAN. "Whether or no, I sometimes—God forgi'e me— laugh wi' horror at the querness o't, till I am that weak I can hardly go round house. He should have the washing of 'em a few times; I warrant 'a wouldn't want to eat babies any more."

Thomas Hardy

So the people of threatened England move and talk. They speak in ghosts of words. All under the passage of time seems so tiny and dim that the squeaks of villagers and Emperors hardly differ in their value, and when they have said their little say the clouds of oblivion pass over them all alike.

Perhaps unconsciously anticipating, or remembering those passages in the drama about "Europe's wormy dynasties rerobing themselves in their old gilt", and Napoleon's saying that he found the Crown of France in the mire and picked it up at the point of his prevailing sword, I once asked Hardy whether England would not have been better justified in standing beside Napoleon when ridding the world of dynasties and all their trumpery. He answered, "No; on the whole the British cause was the right. Our forefathers could not have allowed Napoleon to include England under his tyranny." He went on to quote one of Wordsworth's great sonnets—the one beginning, "It is not to be thought of that the Flood of British freedom . . . That this most famous stream in Bogs and Sands should perish". And he might well have quoted from a less familiar sonnet, equally applicable to Napoleon's time and to our own 1941. After giving instances of past national trespasses, the verses continue:—

> England! all nations in this charge agree;
> But worse, more ignorant in love and hate,
> Far, far more abject is thine Enemy.
> Therefore the wise pray for thee, though the freight
> Of thy offences be a heavy weight;
> Oh grief, that Earth's best hopes rest all with thee!

It was natural that another and even sterner question was put to Hardy. At the very end of the Epic we find a scene in "The Overworld" and we hear the Spirit of the Years and the

Thomas Hardy

Spirit of the Pities answer each other in detached verse, the
Spirit Ironic once intervening. At the very end there sings a
Chorus, certain of the Pities, perhaps joined in the strain by
the Spirit of the Years in combination:—

> But—a stirring fills the air
> Like to sounds of joyance there
> That the rages
> Of the ages
Shall be cancelled and deliverance offered from the darts
that were,
Consciousness the Will informing, till It fashion all things fair

"I should not write that last line now," said the poet in 1922
as I told at the end of Chapter I. "But why not give us that
gleam of hope, however faint?" he was asked. And he answered
with the one word "Versailles!" Who could say that he was
wrong in estimating all the implications of that fatal word
And yet we may turn again to that other poet with whom
Hardy always had so much in common. Addressing our country
Wordsworth wrote:—

> But dearly must we prize thee; we who find
> In thee a bulwark for the cause of men;
> And I by my affection was beguiled;
> What wonder if a poet now and then,
> Among the many movements of his mind
> Feel for thee as a Lover or a Child!

With those beautiful words in our hearts, we must take
leave of Thomas Hardy, one of the most keenly imaginative
creative, humorous, and profoundly sympathetic natures who
have added a lasting glory to our English literature.